*Printed
For
Quixote Press
by*
BRENNAN PRINTING
*100 Main Street
Deep River, Iowa 52222*
515-595-2000

MINNESOTA'S VANISHING OUTHOUSES

by
Bruce Carlson

QUIXOTE PRESS
R.R. #4, Box 33B
Blvd. Station
Sioux City, Iowa 51109

© 1991 by A. Bruce Carlson

All rights reserved. No part of this book may be reproduced or transmitted in any form or by any means, electronic or mechanical, including photocopying, recording or by any informational storage or retrieval system, except by a reviewer who may quote brief passages in a review to be printed in a magazine or newspaper-without permission in writing from the publisher. For information contact Bruce Carlson, Quixote Press, R.R. #4, Box 33B, Blvd. Station, Sioux City, Iowa 51109.

* * * * * * * * *

QUIXOTE PRESS
Bruce Carlson
R.R. #4, Box 33B
Blvd. Station
Sioux City, Iowa
51109

PRINTED IN U.S.A.

DEDICATION

This book is dedicated to all those Minnesotans who have rushed down those familiar paths to the outhouse on a cold night, only too anxious to get back to the warmth and comfort of their beds.

The author wants to thank all those who have shared information with him to make this book possible.

He wants to thanks those who have told of memories about incidents that made the Minnesota outhouse an important part of their lives.

TABLE OF CONTENTS

FOREWORD 9
PREFACE 11
CHAPTERS
    I JOEY'S BAD DAY 13
    II JUST UNFAIR 19
    III FROM THE TOP DOWN..........25
    IV THE MIX-UP 31
    V A VOICE FROM THE GRAVE 35
    VI MATT'S MISTAKE 41
    VII THE DUAL PURPOSE OUTHOUSE ..47
    VIII THE GLUE JOB 53
    IX DOIN' THINGS BACKWARDS 57
    X WHERE'S THE DOOR.............61
    XI TOO MANY KNOBS 67
    XII REALLY STUCK 71
    XIII HOMEMADE STORMS 77
    XIV THE UNTOLD STORY 81
    XV THE NEW DOORWAY 83
    XVI UPWARD BOUND 87
    XVII WIDE OPEN SPACES 95
    XVIII MISTAKEN IDENTITY.............99
    XIX JUST TOO DANGEROUS 105
    XX THE LAST WORD 115
    XXI THE WRONG TRAGET 121
    XXII THE TREE OUTHOUSE 127
    XXIII STUFFED SHIRT 133
    XXIV THE DEEP CHILL 143
    XXV NO MEAT.....................151
EPILOGUE 157
INDEX 163

FOREWORD

The human experience is strewn with artifacts, institutions, and ideas that have each served their purpose, then faded into obscurity. These have varied from the trivial to the notable, and from the base to the noble.

Such has been the lot of the outhouse here in Minnesota. Someday the last outhouse in the state will be pushed into a creek or fall victim to a bonfire. That day will be both as important and as unnoticed as the day the first outhouse was built among the prairie grasses of Minnesota. Drum rolls and the waving of flags will no more accompany the demise of the last than they did the birth of the first. It will happen quietly. Most ideas come and go that way.

The end of the outhouse is probably a good thing. We have better ways now. However, those of us who have lived with The-Little-House-Out-Back will always have a little warm spot in our hearts for that ugly little structure. If nothing else, it sure did a great job of making us appreciate indoor plumbing.

Professor Phil Hey
Briar Cliff College
Sioux City, Iowa

PREFACE

This is a book about the vanishing outhouses of Minnesota. It has some illustrations and stories about those little houses out back that have played such a pivotal role in the life of early Minnesota.

Some of the outhouses spoken of in this book are still in use, but many now serve no more important function than sheltering things like fence posts that really don't need to be sheltered. Some are reduced to being roosting places for sparrows, or simply lean against a nearby boxelder tree, jus' kinda tired, ya know.

I suppose that, someday, the Privius Americanus that ranged the prairies of Minnesota will find itself in a museum where passers-by can look at it among the other relics. But today there are still a few tucked away among the trees and buildings of Minnesota farmsteads. If you want your child or grandchild to see a real live Privius Americanus, you'd better hurry. They are a vanishing species.

The reader must appreciate the fact that, with one or two exceptions, none of these stories have ever been published before. Some of them could cause embarrassment to living people today. Because of that, some of the stories use fictitious names. In those cases, it should be understood that any similarity between those names and actual people, living or dead, is purely coincidental.

CHAPTER I

JOEY'S BAD DAY

There were two circumstances that got Joey Martin into lots of trouble one day. Joey, who lived with his parents and one brother on the outskirts of Minneapolis was basically a good kid, but his halo slipped a little bit back in September of 1912. In fact, it slipped enough to get him in trouble with his parents, his big brother, his teacher, and virtually every girl in school that day. Joey mananged to accomplish that with a couple of indiscretions that fall day.

It started out when the temptation to "borrow" his big brother's brand spankin' new pocket knife got too much for him. That knife was a birthday present, and Joey was pretty well eaten up with envy when Charles got that knife from his father. Before that day was over, Joey wished he'd never seen that knife.

He took the knife to the country school that he reluctantly attended on a semi-regular basis.

As could be expected, the other boys were pretty impressed with the knife. The blade was stout and sharp as a razor.

Joey should have left that thing in his desk which he went up the hill to the outhouse during afternoon recess, but he just couldn't bear the thought of a recess going by without having it to show off.

As he sat there in the outhouse, it occurred to him that he could carve a little peek-hole there in the wall that separated the boys' portion of the school outhouse from the girls'. After all, it sure wouldn't have been the first time that was done. Several little squares of tin nailed over peep-holes gave ample evidence that the idea has occurred to others before Joey.

That sharp blade made short work of the pine board. Our little friend got so engrossed in his illegal task that he didn't even hear someone go into the girls' half of the building. He just kept working that blade around to enlarge that peep-hole.

Meanwhile Janice Woodward in the other side of the wall was surprised and then angered to see what was going on. She didn't know who was carving that hole in the wall, but she knew its purpose. She also figured out an effective way of dealing with the nastly culprit on the other side of the wall.

Janice carefully undid the heavy cast iron coat hook from its place inside the outhouse door. Getting a firm grip on that hook, she brought it down sharply on that busy knife blade. A metallic ping and the sight of the end of the blade lying there on the floor showed her she had succeeded.

A panic stricken "Holly Cow!" coming from across the wall confirmed her success. With a little smile, Janice replaced the coat hook back onto the door and went back out into the playground to see who she had gotten even with.

It didn't take long for the news to travel throughout the playground that Joey Martin had broken the blade of his brother's new knife. A lot of boys stood there surveying the broken knife, feeling sorry for Joey but awfully awfully glad that they weren't in his shoes that day.

Meanwhile the girls all knew exactly what had happened and occupied their time telling each other that nastly little Joey Martin got exactly what he deserved that day. It wasn't a day that made for a whole lot for amiable relations between the boys and the girls in that school.

Joey ended up facing a lot of serious charges. For openers his teacher got him for misconduct. The girls were calling him Nasty Joey Martin. His troubles weren't over when he left school, of course. His brother, Charles, was a world of upset over having his knife broken. Charles had several colorful descriptive words for Joey, not least among them was "thief".

Mrs. Martin was pretty upset about the whole thing. Not only had he taken the knife without permission, but broke it; and did so while on a mission he had no business doing whatsoever.

Joey's father went through the motions of giving him a good chewing out, too. He seemed, however, not to really have his heart in the process. He later confessed to his wife that one of those tin-covered

(16)

holes in that wall was covering a hole that he had made when he was a boy. That, of course, really made Mrs. Martin's day. Now she had two of them in the family to be ashamed of.

On top of everything else, Joey was made to take some money out of his savings to buy Charles another knife.

Eventually the fuss all calmed down, of course. Quite a few years went by for Joey not having to hear any more about that fateful day.

On June 14, 1925, however, he heard all about it again. That was the day he got married. Among all the gifts on the table at the reception was a long narrow one all nicely wrapped. It was from Charles.

Joey had some tall explaining to do to his bride when they unwrapped that gift and found it to be a pine board with a hole in it. Charles had retrieved that board when they tore the outhouse down. He had enjoyed the anticipation of giving it to Joey on his wedding day.

Joey's bride didn't think any more of that little trick than his mother had.

CHAPTER II

JUST UNFAIR

Very often life is basically unfair, unfair to the point of being downright irritating.

So it was with Cy Cooper back in 1922 when he lived just east of Rochester. Cy had been to town and had bought a new pair of boots. For some reason that pair of boots ended up that day on the walk out by the outhouse when Cy got home, instead of in the house where they should have.

Perhaps Cy dropped them there as he went out to the outhouse when he got home that day. Maybe he got to carrying in too much stuff and simply dropped his boots there to lighten his load.

Whatever the cause. Cy Cooper later found those boots setting on that path as he went to the little house out back that evening. Cy was surprised to find those boots there on the path and pleased to see that his mischevious pup hadn't carried one or both of them off. Cy just scooped those boots up and carried them on into the outhouse with him.

"I sure wasn't goin' risk that pup makin' off with them boots there after I'd left 'em layin' out all day that way and gettin' away with it. That damn pup was the worst one for carrying' stuff off. And new boots wuz right expensive, you know."

Cy went on to tell me about the course of events after he took the boots with him into the outhouse.

"I wuz settin' there with those boots on the seat beside me when I brushed again 'em with my arm. Next thing you know I heard one of those dang boots fall. I reached over there in the darkness and felt but one boot."

"Oh, oh!" I said.

"Yep, yer right. I knew those boots was settin' awful close to that second hole in the seat. I got to cussin' and carryin' on. It jus' ain't no fun losin' one boot of a brand new pair, especially down the pit of an old outhouse.

Now, you know some guys have lost things down in outhouse pits and got 'em back. Fact is, my uncle lost his hat down in one of those one day. He got it back, but he eventually had to throw it out anyway. That dang hat stunk like you wouldn't believe it. My Aunt Carrie wouldn't even let my uncle bring that thing in the house. He'd park it outside on a nail for awhile, but he soon gave that up, and simply tossed it."

I sure couldn't see going down in that pit and then have to end up throwing that boot away anyway.

So I decided not to go after that boot, but jus' let 'er be where it was.

Now, ya know, one boot jus' ain't no good at all, no matter how nice and new it is. I was so dang mad, I jus' pitched the other one down there, too. At least, that way, I had the satisfaction of havin' that one useless boot out of sight."

Cy seemed to be getting mad all over again about that loss of all those years ago. I could tell that he was still a bit upset over that. As he told me the rest of the story, I begin to understand why he'd still be bothered about it.

Cy told me about how several days had gone by and he was just beginning to be able to forget his bad luck. He was back in the outhouse, but this time in the full light of day. He was setting there thinking about the various chores he'd have to get done that day. His eyes chanced upon the very end of a shoelace just barely sticking out from under the door that was swung back almost against the wall as it stood open.

With a sinking heart, Cy moved that door out so he could see behind it, afraid of what he would find.

"Sure enough; there it was. There was that boot that had fallen. It had lit down behind the door and

(22)

I had figured it had gone down in the pit. It was dark in there that night, ya know. I sure hadn't knowed it fell down behind the door."

Once again, Cy was faced with the problem of having but one boot in his hands and the other down in the pit. This time, though, the one in the pit was really there.

"So, what'da do?" I asked.

"Well, ya know, one boot ain't no good at all. It don't make no difference how nice and new it is. I jus' pitched 'er down the hole."

Sometimes life just isn't fair at all.

CHAPTER III

FROM THE TOP DOWN

hy is that we tend to do jobs from the top down? When we go to paint a wall or wash a car we start at the top and work on down. We even tend to undress in that manner. A guy will generally take his shirt off before he does his trousers. Then when we dress again, out clothes are likely to be slipped over our head. Trousers and socks are notable exceptions to this, of course.

Sometimes this technique makes sense, and sometimes it doesn't. On occasion it can be downright disasterous. So it was when Keith Walpole put his citified nephew, Brad, to work. Keith found his charge to be almost more trouble than he was worth. He only agreed to take the young man on for the summer because the lad's father, Keith's brother, had almost begged him to do so.

Brad was willing enough but simply didn't know anything about living or working on a farm. The difference between country living and city living in the late 'teens was more pronounced than it is now, of course. The chores there on Keith's farm south of Mankato were almost more than Brad could handle.

Under his breath, Keith would tend to make observations about how useless that young fellow was.

Keith couldn't trust Brad to hoe the garden. The boy didn't know a weed from a watermelon vine. The one time Keith had Brad split some firewood, he almost split his own foot wide open.

One day, through, Keith's eyes fell on the sad-looking roof on the outhouse. Now there was a job that Brad could probably do without getting into too much trouble.

"Do you know how to shingle a roof, lad?"

"Sure do, Uncle Keith. I helped Dad do our garage roof in New Ulm. Dad told me at the time that I did a good job of it, too."

"Well, I got a bundle of nice cedar shingles out in the barn by where we keep the oats for the cows.

Tomorrow you can climb up there on the roof of the outhouse and tear all the old shingles off and put those new ones on."

Keith felt good about Brad knowing how to shingle. It just never hurt to ask, of course.

That next day Keith gave Brad that bundle of shingles, some shingle nails, and told him to go to it. Meanwhile Keith took off for town to run some errands he had.

Things didn't work out quite the way Keith wanted them to in town. When he drove on home, he was much too preoccupied with those concerns to worry much about the roofing job on the outhouse.

It wasn't until that evening when Keith remembered the outhouse project and asked Brad how it was gone. Brad assured his uncle that he had gotten the job done. Keith was glad to hear that and that it had gone well.

By morning Keith had pretty well forgotten the roofing project, and by noon when he went out to the outhouse, that project was forgotten completely.

It was already sprinkling when Keith took off from the kitchen. Within minutes, it was raining like all get out as it can so easily do with a June rain.

Keith had just gotten settled down when the first drops hit hime on the arm. Within moments it was raining inside the outhouse just about as hard as it was on the outside. Keith couldn't believe that was happening. Here, he'd just had Brad reshingle that building yet it was soaking wet inside.

Keith's braving the downpour to go out to investigate wasn't really that much of a sacrifice on his part since it was raining right briskly inside anyway.

What he saw when he stood there in the downpour was enough to make a grown man cry. That dang Brad had started at the top of the roof and worked down with those shingles. The shingles were all overlapped alright, just exactly backwards to what they should have been. Each shingle was going a good job of channeling the rain water under the one below it, thus running it right into the inside of the outhouse.

Keith put Brad to work the next day taking all those nice new shingles off and putting new ones on right. He was scared stiff that one of the neighbors would happen by the house and see those shingles up there on the outhouse, all backwards. One of the neighbors had never let him forget the time that he had poured water in the gas tank of his car. Keith sure didn't need to get all that hassle over the shingles on the outhouse.

CHAPTER IV

THE MIX-UP

o this day Frank Hopewell and Adrian Metcalf are good friends. They often joke about the day in 1938 though when Frank came to work for Adrian as a hired man on the Metcalf farm north of Austin.

Adrian was a young farmer who took Frank on as a hired man for "a few days." Those few days grew into months, and eventually Frank became

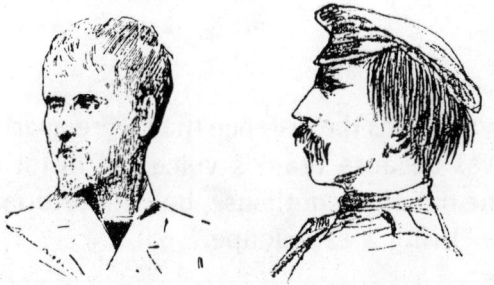

Adrian's partner on that farm. Neither of the men ever married so the relationship lasted for over half

a century. These men both live in a retirement home in Minneapolis today.

That first day back in 1938 was almost the last one though. Both Frank and Adrian had good reason to question just what sort of person the other was on that day.

It all started when Frank started work that morning. By midmorning he found it necessary to retire to the outhouse. While out there, however, he found the mail order catalog was gone.

Since the outhouse was near the back door of the house and Frank knew that Adrian was in the kitchen, he hollered at him to "Bring a catalog."

Maybe it was the distance they were apart. Maybe it was because Frank's voice got distorted as it came out of the outhouse, but what Adrian heard was "Bring a cantaloupe."

Now Adrian wasn't the kind of guy to meddle in another man's business, but he thought that Frank wanting a cantaloupe while out there in the outhouse was a bit odd. He wondered just what sort of fellow his new hired man was.

Frank, on the other hand, was shocked when Adrian's arm poked through the door bearing a cantaloupe. For lack of knowing what else to do, Frank took the thing and wondered why his new boss would do that.

However, Frank stayed the day and ended up staying a good many years. Perhaps the fact that both Frank and Adrian were avid collectors of Indian artifacts kept them together in spite of the concern each had about the other.

It was about a week later when the pair were sitting out on the porch during a rain that the reason for that first day's incident occurred to Adrian. He started to laugh so hard he could barely bring himself to tell Frank why he took him a cantaloupe that day.

"I thought you said "cantaloupe, but it was "catalog" you said, wasn't it?"

CHAPTER V

A VOICE FROM THE GRAVE

Maybe it's my imagination, but there seems to be quite a few of these outhouse stories that involve a ghost. But then again, maybe I'm just attuned to ghost stories because I've written some books about them.

But anyway, this is one of those that involves a ghost, or at least what Phil Weaver thought was a ghost.

It all started the day Phil visited the old home place near Faribault. That visit to his brother and his family was sort of a trip down Memory Lane for Phil. He was born and had been raised on that place and had a lot of memories about it.

Phil and Guy's parents had both passed away and the two boys were well into middle age in the late 1920s when all this happened.

Guy's family still used the outhouse that had served the family for decades. It was the same one that Phil remembered being there on the place when he was a child.

As Phil was settin' out in that familiar little shack that evening just about dark, his mind was reaching back many years. His two little nieces playing around the house earlier that day reminded him of how all the kids in their family used to play together. He recalled how he and Guy used to stick chicken feathers into the soft center of a corn cob and throw the whole thing high in the air. Those corncobs would come whirling back to earth if the feathers would be positioned just right. He thought about how the two of them would do that for hour after hour, never tiring of it. He recalled with a smile of how his sister had a fancy little doll buggy she would haul her dolls around in, and how he had swiped that buggy once to give his pet pig a ride.

"I'm going to have to tell her about that some time. I think it's safe now." he thought to himself.

Phil hadn't been aware of exactly what those two nieces of his had been playing that day. He was unaware that little Molly and her older sister were playing house.

Molly really enjoyed that because when she was the "mother" she could order her big sister around.

Neither did Phil know that the girls had one of those old-fashioned tin can telephones rigged up between the outhouse and their bedroom upstairs. Those two tin cans with the taunt string connecting them did a pretty good job of enabling the pair to "visit" on their telephone back and forth from their bedroom to the outhouse.

All the elements were falling into place. Phil was out there in the outhouse lost in thought about his childhood. The tin can telephone was there overhead, unknown to Phil.

The girls were playing in their room when Amy, the older sister, took off for the outhouse and Molly decided to call her on that tin can telephone. She waited a couple of minutes until she figured her sister was in the outhouse and then put her mouth to the tin can to talk to Amy. Their playing house earlier in the day led her to think of something in that vein to say.

Meanwhile Amy saw the outhouse door was closed so she knew someone was already in there. She had started back to the house and had gotten as far as the back porch when Molly talked into that tin can.

"Come, your mother want's you!"

Those were probably the last five words Phil Weaver expected to hear coming out of nowhere.

The distortion of Molly's voice coming through that toy telephone was enough to make it sound kind of hollow and garbled, but not enough to mask the similarity of her voice to that of her grandmother's. Phil thought it was his mother's voice, calling him to join her.

Amy was the next person to be very surprised. She had gotten to the porch when suddenly the door of the outhouse burst open and her uncle came out of there like he'd been shot.

Amy stood shocked into immobility as Phil rushed by her for the safety of the kitchen. She said later she could think of nothing but how odd it was to see the door of the outhouse swing out when it was made to swing in.

That door opened outward to the accompanyment of crashing wood for Phil Weaver that night, when he heard what he thought to be a voice from the grave.

CHAPTER VI

MATT'S MISTAKE

Speaking of graves, there was a gravedigger up around Minneapolis who lost his contracts with several of the local churches for digging graves in their cemeteries. It was all due to a mistake in judgment he made about outhouses.

Traditionally grave diggers plied their trade on only a part-time basis. Their equipment usually consited only of a spade or a shovel. It wasn't high-tech operation at all. This particular gravedigger,

however, had a fancy piece of equipment for the job and pursued it full time.

His machine was on four wheels and he'd pull it

(41)

from cemetery to cemetery with a team of horses. Once he got it positioned on the plot, however, a gasoline engine would take over to do the digging of the hole. That machine would dig a nice squared-off hole exactly seven feet long, four feet wide, and six feet deep. It was such an ingenuous machine and so much fun to watch with all its gears and belts that Matt would sometimes charge extra for folks to watch it do its thing.

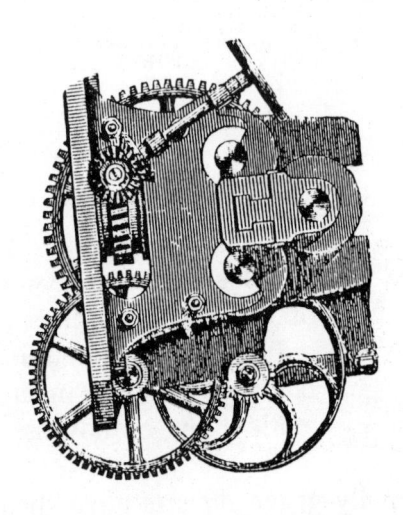

All in all, it was a pretty easy way to make a living there in Minneapolis for Matt Johnson since many of the local churches used his services.

While there was enough work to keep him busy, he got to thinking that if he could put that machine to work on other things, he could do better than simply make a decent living. As he thought about that, it occurred to him that with a little modification, he could adapt that machine to dig a hole about four feet square and advertise for work digging outhouse pits.

After tinkering around with that thing for a few days, he found he had a perfect outhouse pit digger.

Matt was right when he figured that there would be lots of folks who would hire him to dig those outhouse pits. Within a short time, he found a nice little supplement to his normal income. He couldn't make enough digging those pits to make a living at it, but it sure promised to be a nice little extra.

Matt should have stuck with his gravedigging business and not wandered off into digging outhouse pits. Some of the ladies in one of the churches got wind of the news that Matt was digging outhouse pits with the very same machine he used to dig graves. That was just too much for that particular bunch of ladies, and they brought their influece to bear on the church officials to serve notice on Matt that thereafter they would get their gravedigging done by someone else.

Well now, if that wasn't bad enough, some of the other churches did the same thing. Folks figured that if that machine got used for such an undignified purpose, it wasn't good enough to dig graves in their cemeteries.

If Matt had been thinking fast enough, he probably could have reversed the tide flowing against him by swearing off the outhouse pit digging and concentrating on digging graves. However, as he was mulling that all over, he got out-foxed by another fellow. That guy went out and got him one of those fancy machines like Matt had and went into the grave-digging business.

This new competition out maneuvered Matt by doing just the opposite of what Matt had done. He added a touch of class by running his machine while he was all dressed up in a suit, a fancy coat, and a top hat. He also painted his machine a snow white. This dignified looking fellow all duded up and with his snow white machine made a much better impression on people than grubby old Matt Johnson with his old greasy machine.

This new fellow was more than a gravedigger. He also was a good salesman and knew that he could succeed by excelling where Matt was weakest.

In spite of the fact that he charged quite a bit more than Matt had, he soon had a thriving business going. He had the same customers that Matt had had, plus quite a few new ones who were impressed with his "professional" air.

Counterattacking too late with too little, Matt visited quite a few of the more influencial members of the various churches, but it was to no avail. He had lost his business and it was gone for good. His willingness to come in at a price considerably lower than that fellow with the top hat meant nothing to the folks in Minneapolis. They had a professional now and weren't about to go back to old Matt with his greasy old machine that had been used to dig outhouse pits.

The source of this story told me that Matt finally solved his problem by taking his machine somewhere out west where folks were unaware of his little indescretion.

CHAPTER VII

THE DUAL PURPOSE OUTHOUSE

Glen Axelman was pretty heavy into fishing. He had gotten bitten by the fishing bug early in life and never got over it.

Like many other avid fisherman he wouldn't quit just because winter came. He was as willing to fish through the ice as he was when the weather was warm. Glen didn't particularly care to eat 'em, but he was all for catchin' 'em.

Like other ice fisherman, Glen had a shelter to protect him from the elements. Since he lived near the Mississippi River just northwest of Red Wing, it was handy to do his ice fishing out there on the river.

Glen's shelter was a bit unique. Come ice fishing time, he'd hook his team up to the outhouse and

drag it out onto the ice. It was kind of a handy arrangement. He could sit in there and fish right throught the holes in the seat. It worked real well, and Glen was right proud of the idea.

There were a couple or problems associated with the whole plan. One was his and the other was the other guys who were ice fishing. None of these people thought it was a particularly good idea for Glen to be using that outhouse; but for different reasons.

Mrs. Axelman felt it was a bit beyond the call of normal marital responsibilities to have do without an outhouse for a good portion of the winter. Glen's contention was that there were plenty of woods around that could be used for those few winter months.

"Winters here are pretty short, don't ya know. It's not like we wuz up in Canada somewheres that they got long winters."

All that, of course, failed to make much of an impression on Mrs. Axelman. She persisted in the strange notion that she should have access to an outhouse year around.

The other fisherman, on the other hand, could have cared less about the availability, or lack thereof, of such facilities at the Axelman home. Their contention was that one of them using an outhouse for an ice fishing shack made them all look a little bit weird. Few of those fellows relished the idea of being considered to be in the same league with Glen Axelman anyway.

All in all, Glen was a bit of at a loss why everyone was making such a fuss over what seemed to be a very logical answer to his need for an ice fishing shack.

This rather contentious situation lasted for several years until 1911 when Glen's shack burned to the ground; or rather, the ice. It happened at night. Since there hadn't been a fire in the stove in there for several days, it was generally considered to have been a case of arson. That caused a lot of talk among the local folks for quite a few days, of course.

The boys at the general store let it be known that there was "talk" of Glen's shack probably catching on fire again if what he brought down to replace the first one was also an outhouse.

Glen didn't need to have it spelled out to him. He could see that the fellows were determined that he wasn't going to have an outhouse there on the ice. He figured while that was a good idea, he simply couldn't continue with it.

Having to build a regular ice fishing shack kind of galled old Glen, especially when he knew that one or more of those scoundrels were the cause of it, but that's what he did.

The replacement shack was a rather ordinary one, looking no different than any of the many others out there on the Mississippi River.

Glen almost stumbled onto the truth one evening and didn't even suspect it. He was out on the back porch ratting through a pile of old boots and overshoes, looking for a pair of gloves he had lost.

While doing that he came across a pair of his wife's overshoes that reeked of kerosene. When he asked her why her books smelled so badly of kerosene, she thought her role in the loss of the outhouse was discovered. She came up with some lame excuse about how a leaky kerosene lamp had spilled out onto them.

Glen bought that story, never suspecting that she had sloshed some kerosene on them the night she walked out to the outhouse at midnight and burnt it down.

CHAPTER VIII

THE GLUE JOB

Speaking of problems with your wife, that's exactly what Jim Vance had one day many years ago over an outhouse incident.

Vance's outhouse there at their home near Owatonna was a bit fancier than most. It was not only painted inside, but had a rug and wallpaper. The seats were far from simple holes cut in a wide pine board. They had regular store-bought seats with lids. The seats were nailed to the pine board and the lid was hinged, of course. The whole arrangement looked much like a modern bathroom, minus the plumbing, of course.

Jim didn't set out that day to get into hot water with his wife, but he sure managed to do it. He had decided to give the entire inside of the outhouse a new paint job. He not only did the woodwork but also the cabinet and dry sink they had in there. Unfortunately, Jim choose to use an oil-based glossy enamel that got as tough as rawhide after it dried.

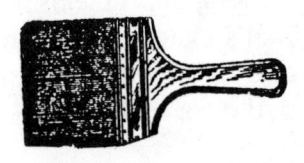

Jim had enough sense to know that he'd have to paint the inside of the lid on one pass and the outside on another since the lid would have to be either up or down, resting on the seat or against the wall. He knew that one side had to be done and then allowed to dry before doing the other.

Knowing something, however, and remembering it every time are different things altogether.

As luck would have it, Jim forget that little detail on that project. The inevitable result was that the lid ended up glued tight as could be to the seat.

Now that's the kind of situation that can be downright disasterous under the wrong conditions. And the wrong conditions happened, of course. When Mrs. Vance went out to the outhouse the next day, she found the lid glued down so tight to the seat that it might as well been bolted there.

The Vances' son, Al, who told me this story, didn't know how his mother solved her problem, but he did know that his father got a good chewing out for that dumb move.

Apparently, she made enough of an impression on Jim that he never pulled that little trick again.

CHAPTER IX

DOIN' THINGS BACKWARDS

The old gent in a rest home in St. Paul who told me this story could hardly get his attention focused on the story. He got all hyped about what was obviously a favorite theme of his. It had to do with where people ate and where they went to the bathroom.

"Why, it's the dangest thing ya ever saw," he loudly complained to me within two minutes of my meeting him.

"Ya got folks these days adoin' things just backwards."

My asking what he meant was almost pointless. It was obvious he was going to expound on his position and didn't really need any encouragement from me.

"Why, when I was a young feller, folks had enough sense to do things right."

"How's that?" I asked.

"Well, only good sense tells ya that you are 'sposed to eat inside and go to the bathroom outside! But, what'll they do now? They do it 'xacely backwards. They eat outside and go to the outhouse inside. Why, it ain't even an outhouse!

It's a bathroom. Nosiree, I see no sense to it. They can call 'em picnics, 'er bar-b-ques, or whatever. Whatever they call 'em don't make no difference. You're 'sposed to eat inside and 'nother thing. You're 'sposed to go to the bathroom outside.

Now this seemed like an issue hardly worth getting all fired up over, but this old man seemed to have a real thing about it. He got so caught up in the issue I had trouble getting the story out of him that his grandson said he had.

After a few stabs at getting his story, he finally got around to telling it to me.

The old man's story was about the time when he was a little kid. Unfortunately for him, he was the low man on the family totem pole since he was the youngest boy. Whenever anything had to be done that was distasteful, his older brothers would force him to do it.

So it was one day when one of the bigger boys lost his wallet down in the outhouse pit. Guess who was chosen to go after it? His brothers tied a rope onto him and lowered him down into that pit so he could retrieve that wallet.

"So, did you get the wallet back?" I asked.

"Sure did, but it wasn't a pleasant job; you can bet on that."

As I felt the old duffer, I could sympathize with how that, indeed, must have been an unpleasant task. I also couldn't help but wonder why, after that experience, he had such an affection for those outhouses. After that, I would have thought he'd see all kinds of advantages to eating outside and going to the bathroom inside.

CHAPTER X

WHERE'S THE DOOR?

These next four stories are all accounts of practical jokes played on occupants of outhouses.

Now, one learns to expect boys to pull dumb tricks on people, but somehow, we expect girls to have a little more sense. Such was not the case, however, with a situation at a rural tavern not too far from Worthington.

This tavern had the traditional pair of outhouses out back. There was also a pair of twin girls there; daughters of the owner of the place. Lorriane and Louise Clante were in their teens when they found they could provide themselves with lots of entertainment at the expense of their father's male clientile there at the tavern.

The trick these girls pulled was one that was both simple and effective.

What the pair did was to replace the outhouse door with one whose boards were made of the same siding as covered the rest of the outhouse. The outside of the door had a handle and was painted a different color than the wall, so it was obviously the entry to the building and could be easily recognized as such.

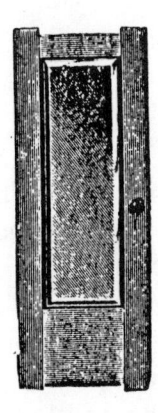

The inside of that door was an entirely different situation, however. The vertital space between it and the adjacent siding was masked by the two-by-four studding. The color was the same and there was no handle or other hardware on it whatsoever.

So, when that door was closed, it was totally indistinguable from the rest of the wall when viewed from the inside.

Then to compound the situation, the girls hung another door on the inside of the outhouse that was hinged and had a handle. That door led nowhere. You could open it all you wanted. All there was on the other side was a blank wall.

What the girls really wanted to do was to have the fake door a real exit and lead into the neighboring women's outhouse, but their father drew the line on that.

(62)

The regular patrons of the tavern had been in that outhouse enough that they knew what was going on. They knew they could get out again simply by pushing on what appeared to be a blank wall. They knew that the obvious way out of the building led to nowhere. Even they, however, would forget on occasion and try that door there on the inside of the outhouse.

Strangers in the tavern, however, were fair game. The girls both worked for their father in the tavern so would alert each other when a stranger would head out for the outhouse.

Being on the road between Worthington and Jackson, Mr. Clante's tavern hosted some pretty fancy travelers on occasion. The fancy gentlemen with the citified ways were the ones the girls like to catch the most in their trick. They would always seem to get the most upset over it.

The poor victims of these innocent looking girls would invariably and repeatedly attempt to get out of their unexpected prison by opening and closing that door and banging away at it.

Meanwhile the girls would be sitting at their bedroom window above the outhouse and comment to each other about the state of mind of the poor soul below. Some of the fellows would remember exactly how they got into the building and push on that wall, thus getting back out. Others were totally fooled by the situation and would take quite a while getting out again. On a couple of occasions, Mr. Clante would have to go out and release them.

The situation could be difficult enough when a man was cold sober. When he had a few drinks, it could be even worse. Those fellows often got out by discovering the real exit by accident by falling against it.

These folks who had had a few too many would often come back into the tavern and rail loud and hard against Mr. Clante for their having been so tricked. Surprisingly enough, however, Mr. Clant let the girls have their fun. My source for this story was of the opinion that he enjoyed the whole thing as much as the girls did.

The girls kept their joke going for several years, catching a couple of hundred victims over that time.

Lorraine kept it going even after Louise got married and left the tavern, but would tell Louise of some of the fellows their trap would snare.

Eventually, however, all good things must end. So it was with the trick outhouse. The end of that little joke come one day when a gentleman fell victim to the joke and became very upset over it. This man, after he got out, made careful note of the location of the tavern and Mr. Clante's name. As he left, he advised Mr. Clante that he would be bringing the law down on him. That was the end of the trick outhouse.

CHAPTER XI

TOO MANY KNOBS

A similar trick to that in the previous story was one perpetrated by Carroll Jenkins who had an outhouse behind his gasoline station on the Anoka road out of St. Paul many years ago.

Carroll's trick also dealt with his dilemma of how to get out of an outhouse when the way was not obvious. And, like the Clante girls, he went to a lot of effort for the sole purpose of making it difficult for his customers to extract themselves from the outhouse once they were in there. And also, like the Clant girls, he did this by rigging the door.

What Carroll did was to mount a latch set on the door. This was an ordinary knob and latch arrangement. There was one odd thing about it, however. He mounted it about a foot from the floor so a person would have to reach way down in order to unlatch the door. Then, to add an element of confusion, Carrol mounted eleven more such latch sets up and down the same edge of the door. These sets were all alike, but only one of them engaged with the door frame. The rest did nothing other than confuse the occupant. The victim in the outhouse would be held captive until he stumbled onto the right knob, and turned it.

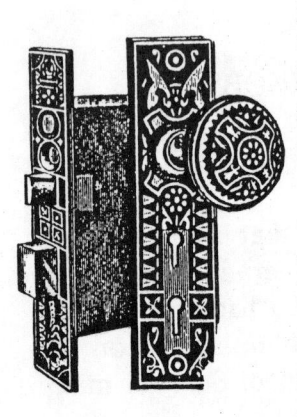

Carroll had somehow ended up with a full case of these latch sets and decided that this was a good way to put them to use.

Carroll took great delight in watching the faces of his customers as they would re-emerge from his outhouse, sometimes after a good deal of knob turning before they would find the right one.

Oftentimes some of the regular loafers or customers who were at the station at the time that someone would go into the outhouse would take bets among themselves as to the time it would take someone to get back out of the outhouse.

Carroll toyed with the idea of having two of those latch sets actually engage with the door frame, thus requiring that the victim not only know that he

(68)

was supposed to turn two of them at a time, but also burden him with the need to pick the right combination of two out of the twelve there on the door.

He gave up on that idea, however, when one of the loafers figured out the mathamatical odds of accidently getting the right combination. Carrol decided he'd have to send lunch in to the poor fellows if he did that.

CHAPTER XII

REALLY STUCK

This story is about another trick that was pulled in an outhouse. This one, however, was done only one time. The joker who did it got all the chewing out he needed from that one time, so decided not to try it a second time.

This little incident took place in an outhouse located in one of Minnesota's state parks, and relatively recently. It was in the summer of 1979.

The whole thing started with a church youth group from St. Cloud that were visiting a park for a week.

One of the boys, Brad Coe, made the mistake of bringing along a small bottle of that new kind of glue that would stick almost anything to almost anything. This stuff would stick something so tight to skin that either the object or the skin had to give. The glue wouldn't.

Brad didn't have any particular use in mind for that fascinating stuff, but he felt that some opportunity would present itself that would afford lots of fun with it.

Brad's "opportunity" turned out to be the idea of putting a small drop of it on the seat of the outhouse. He thought it would be all kinds of funny to have one of his buddies sit down on that glue.

Brad made two mistakes that day. One of them was putting that stuff on the seat and the other was telling several of his friends what he had done. The second mistake is what got him caught doing the first one. When one of the guys sat down on that seat and found himself instantly glued to it, everyone knew who did it.

The poor fellow in the outhouse had a real problem. He was so thoroughly glued to the seat he simply couldn't get up without fear of leaving some of his behind behind.

After an appropriate amount of hollering for help and dire threats against whoever had done that, one of the adult supervisors took charge.

This fellow soon determined the nature of the problem and, after some inquires, also determined who had done the dirty deed.

This particular supervisor was chosen to accompany the boys on the outing because he took no foolishness off anyone and the boys had a lot of respect for the man.

When Brad Coe realized that he was in trouble with Mr. Caseman, he realized he was in lots of trouble.

Mr. Caseman allowed Brad to stew in his own juice while he proceeded to extradite the boy in the outhouse from his predicament. A keyhole saw was obtained from the park attendant and a chunk of that outhouse seat was sawed away to free the boy. The victim, Mr. Caseman, the attendant, and a very contrite Brad Coe all went to town to find a doctor.

Medical help was found and the process of freeing the boy from that chunk of outhouse was started. That consisted of some careful and delicate snipping away of the glue between that little chunk of wood and its prisioner. That was accompained by an occasional yelp of pain. Each outburst reminded Brad of what he probably had coming when that kid would get him alone. It wasn't a pleasant prospect to contemplate. The kid was considerably bigger than Brad and would undoubtedly get his revenge.

Brad ended up coming out of the whole mess pretty lucky. His parents had to come up with the money to pay for the doctor's work and the boy's retaliation was pretty much limited to a few threats that he never carried out.

In addition, Brad got a royal chewing out from Mr. Caseman, the park attendant, and the doctor. These various people took turns working him over until he was thoroughly impressed on the wisdom of not messing with that stuff anymore.

Brad had just about forgotten the incident by the time the week was up and it was time to go home. Unfortunately his father wasn't quite so willing to forget the mess his kid had gotten into at camp and met Brad with the announcement that he was going to have to get a job for the balance of the summer so he could pay his parents back for the cost of the office call to the doctor. He was also informed that he could pay them back for the cost of going to that camp for a week.

CHAPTER XIII

HOMEMADE STORMS

The last of these four stories involving practical jokes is about a young fellow who lived near Bemidji back in the 1920s. This fellow's little trick was made possible by the fact that they had running water on the place at the time, but still didn't have a bathroom.

This particular kid was intrigued by the new toy afforded by their getting running water at their home. He found endless numbers of things he could do with a hose. Some of these things got his hide tanned on occasion, but that was simply the price he had to pay for all that fun. Tanned hides came with the territory of being a boy, and he was used to it.

Young Bill Romey went way beyond the ordinary things

that boys would do like making rainbows in the sunlight or watering down the cat when it got to acting too uppity.

Bill lit onto the idea of making any occupant of the outhouse think it was raining.

It was a simple, but effective trick. Bill found a piece of scrap tin that had been used as a piece of patching material for the chicken coop roof. With a little practice Bill found out he could wiggle that sheet of tin back and forth and make it sound exactly like thunder.

Bill would arm himself with a strong flashlight, his piece of tin, and the garden hose. So prepared, he would wait for someone to go into the outhouse. The Romeys had enough company that Bill rarely had to wait long for a victim.

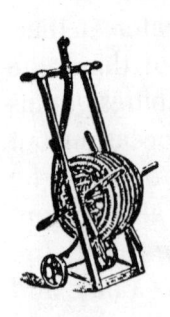

Bill would wait for his prey to get good and settled down in there, then he would sneak up near the building and very softly buckle that sheet of tin back and forth real slowly so it would sound like thunder way off in the distance. Then he'd spray a few drops of water from his hose onto the roof of the outhouse.

Bill would then wait a few seconds before doing it again, but this time louder and using more water.

He would pause but a very short time and then work that piece of tin for all it was worth. At the same time he'd sweep that flashlight beam back and forth near the bottom of the door and the sill. Meanwhile he would train that hose up in the air so the water would come cascading down on the tin roof of that outhouse.

Bill would keep this up for however long it took his prey to dash out of the outhouse for a mad run to the house to avoid getting totally soaked in what he was convinced was a violent summer rainstorm.

All this was the most fun, of course, when it would be a perfectly clear and sunny day. Bill enjoyed the bewilderment that his victims expressed when they would emerge from the outhouse into the bright out-of-doors where there was absolutely no evidence of rain.

CHAPTER XIV

THE UNTOLD STORY

Then there is the story that I'm not even going to tell you. It's about the time that Mel Washburn's dog somehow got hold of the catalog out of Mel's outhouse back in '04 south and east of Fergus Falls.

Before Mel retreived it near the steps to the back porch, that dang dog had drug that catalog through the poison ivy patch down by the chicken coop. Fact is, he must have mauled that catalog around pretty well in that ivy patch.

By the time every body got alright again, Mel sure wished that he had pitched that catalog and gotten a new one.

But like I say, I'm not going to tell you the story. It's too awful to even think about.

CHAPTER XV

THE NEW DOORWAY

Speaking of kicking out a wall of an outhouse, that also happened down near Albert Lea back in 1916.

Ida and Rolfe Jansen lived there near Albert Lee along a little creek. Ida was a large raw-boned woman who could just do a man's work on the farm. She had been raised on a neighboring farm and had had to do the jobs normally reserved for boys. She and her sister didn't have any brother's so they learned early how to work hard.

Strong and tough as Ida was, she had a thing about birds. She was scared stiff of any bird and would almost panic if one got too close. This little quirk of hers had little practical effect on their farming enterprise there near Albert Lee. About the only thing was that they didn't have any chickens. They adjusted to that, however, by trading honey from their bees for dressed chickens. Ida could eat 'em alright. She just couldn't handle them when they were alive.

Sometimes there seems to be a force loose in the world that contrives to make the circumstances just as wrong as they can be. So it was with the Jensen place one night in 1916. That barn owl had chosen the Jensen outhouse to roost in that night. It had to be Ida that went out there instead of George. That silly owl couldn't cooperate by simply flying away. He had to make a big fuss and flop all around inside the outhouse, looking for the door that had been open when he entered the building earlier.

All Ida knew was that the air seemed to be filled with a huge feathered creature. She could feel those wings brushing by her face and even feel the air as the poor owl frantically fluttered around in there looking for that doorway. A large bird fluttering around in a small building can seem to be everywhere at once, of course.

Within a few seconds the owl found an opening big enough for him to fly out of. The bird probably neither knew nor cared that it was a brand new opening. Ida crashed out through the wall, not even bothering to open the door. After it was all over, she didn't even remember breaking out that wall. All she could recall was the terror of being shut up in that little outhouse with a huge bird.

CHAPTER XVI

UPWARD BOUND

Yet today, in 1991, we can still see an occasional old windmill uselessly turning in the breeze in old abandoned homesites where a family once lived. Sometimes the driveshaft that hangs down from the top has been broken or taken off and the blades turn, but move nothing. On occasion that steel drive shaft is still engaged up there at the top and will slowly move up and down as the wind turns the blades. Watching those shafts busy working away on a breezy day but accomplishing nothing is kind of sad.

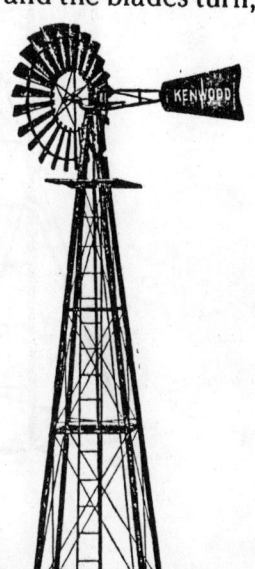

But, on with the outhouse story. This is a story about a farmer near St. Cloud who had to build a new outhouse in the late 1930s after the old one got so rotten it wouldn't even stand up anymore.

This guy was one of the first in the neighborhood to get electricity, so the windmill on his place was already obsolete. The farmer felt that there was no point in letting that nice set of good square and strong legs on that windmill go to waste. He'd simply use those legs as the four corners of his new outhouse. All he'd have to do is put some siding on and a roof, and he'd be in business.

So, that's what he did. It was kind of a funny-looking outhouse, what with the four corners slanted inward a little bit toward the top, but it was good enough for him.

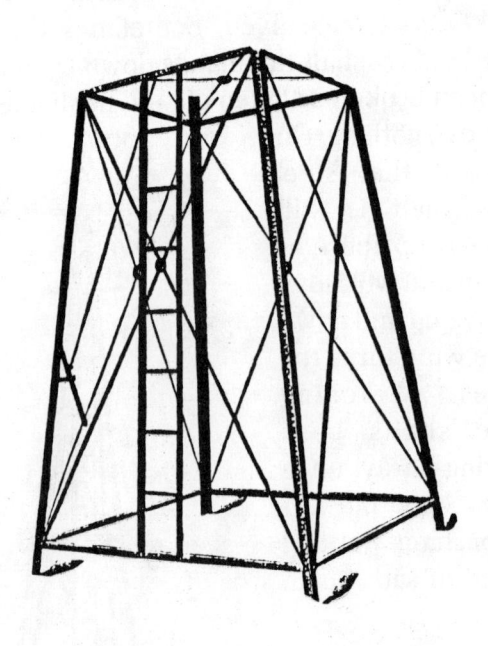

that steel drive shaft still hung down, kind of in the way. The fellow had intended to climb up and disconnect it, but chickened out on that chore. It was long way up there and just as far down if he happened to fall. He simply made a little adjustment in how he built the roof, and allowed that shaft to hang down through it into the center of the outhouse.

Every time the wind came up, that shaft would simply move up and down, but that was no problem. It didn't have any bolts or fittings sticking out of it to catch on a guy's clothes, so it wasn't really in the way. The old duffer got so used to it hanging there in the middle of the outhouse that he didn't really notice it anymore after a while.

But, one Saturday afternoon the local preacher came to see the old farmer to convince him he should be coming to church.

The old duffer was just enough interested that the good preacher felt he was just a smidgon away from getting the farmer to make the plunge into church goin'.

The preacher worked hard getting the fellow to commit to showing up in church the next morning. Because of that, he stayed a lot longer than he had anticipated and found it necessary to make a trip to the "little house out back."

The good reverend was so worked up about getting the man as a new perishioner that he didn't really notice much about the outhouse out there. It was also getting dark enough that he didn't see that the little building was actually built out of the base of a windmill. Except for a steel shaft sticking down out of the roof, the fellow had no reason to think that this particular outhouse was any different than any other.

The preacher did say later that he recalled wondering, for a moment, what that steel shaft was all about.

Anyway, the preacher was setting there and got to realizing that it was getting late, so he had better be on the road. Just then, a sudden breeze came up. That windmill blade high overhead started turning, setting that shaft in motion. The shaft slowly started its downward stroke, at the end of which, it would start up again, of course.

The preacher didn't know about all that. All he knew was that that big shaft sticking down into the outhouse suddenly wasn't in the same position. It didn't occur to him that the shaft was moving downward. He was sure as could be that he and the outhouse were moving upward.

Now, this preacher had mentioned in hundreds of sermons that the promise awaiting all of us who behaved was going to be a journey skyward. He should have been psychologically prepared for it, as much as he had talked about it. Apparently, however, it looked much better on paper than for real. He had no interest in becoming airborne that evening, with or without an outhouse.

All this passed through his mind in a couple of seconds as it appeared the outhouse was rising up. Those couple of seconds were all it took for the person to react. He wanted out and he wanted out a whole lot faster than it would take for him to find the door there in the increasing darkness and get it opened. He recalled that it had closed with some difficulty, as it had scrapped the floor, and he had had to push hard on it to get it closed behind him. He knew he didn't have time to mess with that door, so he made a new doorway. The good man came busting out the flimsy side of the outhouse, not really knowing how far he'd have to fall since he didn't have a good idea of how far up in the air the structure had gotten.

It was, as they say, a moment of truth. He would have to suffer whatever injuries that fate had in store for him. He knew that every second he waited, he would be that much farther up in the air and have that much farther to fall.

The preacher was both surprised and gratified to find that he was still on the ground. This was, though, a bit confusing since he was sure that he was at least a few feet up in the air when he came out of that wall.

The farmer who came rushing out when he heard the ominous sound of splintering wood wasn't what you would call gratified. He was surprised alright, but sure wasn't very thrilled to see one whole wall of his new outhouse laying there on the ground in hunks and splinters.

"What in tarnation is goin' on here, Parson? I heard this terrible sound out here and get here to find you layin' there on the ground and my outhouse in shambles."

"What . . . . ., How can this be? I know sure as I'm laying here that this here outhouse started off up in the sky somehow. I thought sure that the end had come, and I was goin' skyward. I got out as soon as I could. I'm sure sorry for what I did to your outhouse."

Just about that time, the parson saw that the outhouse had been built on the legs of a windmill and figured out what had happened.

All the parson's attempts to explain how sorry he was didn't do any good. The old farmer flat out told him he wouldn't be coming to church the next day, or any other Sunday. He told the preacher that if he was a preacher and didn't know an outhouse from a golden chariot, he probably didn't know much else either.

CHAPTER XVII

WIDE OPEN SPACES

John Penny lived on a farm between Blooming Prairie and Austin. This fellow had a bad case of claustraphobia.

His problem wasn't so severe that it got in the way very much in his farming. Oh, he'd have to get someone else to do his really close work like repairing the cistern or anything involving crawling under buildings. He got along pretty well in spite of his fear of small and confined spaces. As long as he could be out in the open, he was alright.

One thing that John couldn't handle was the prospect of going into an outhouse. Using an outhouse even with the door standing open was really more than he could take. The idea of closing the door and being confined in such a tiny space was more than he even wanted to think about.

Now, a fellow can't do a decent job of farming or anything else if he's burdened all the time with the problem of an outhouse too cramped to be tolerable. It's not like the infrequent need to do repair work on a cistern or work under a building. A fellow uses the outhouse every day of the year and can't let that pose a problem.

John's answer was as simple as it was effective. He simply built him an outhouse with three sides. The whole front of the thing was left open. He had it facing away from the road, so privacy was no real problem.

As an accommodation to anyone else using the outhouse, he did rig up a wall-sized door on a steel track so that front could be closed. John, however, would leave that door rolled wide open so he could have that much more open space in front of him.

The remains of John's outhouse are still standing. The door has long since rusted fast to its track, and the structure now contains nothing more valuable than a pile of old rotten harness and some steel fence posts.

For a lot of years, though, that outhouse served John well.

CHAPTER XVIII

MISTAKEN IDENTITY

As a result of doing the research for this book, I discovered an interesting fact. I discovered that a lot of exciting and memberable things happened in outhouses that were direct results of those little structures not having any lights in them.

Of course, that is understandable. The days when folks used those buildings were, very often, the days when they had no electricity. This meat that they would have to have lamps or candles out there for light. That, of course, was a lot of trouble to go to since there wasn't a lot of reason to have lights out in the outhouse anyway.

By way of compensating for the lack of lighting facilities in outhouses, many people would paint the interiors white so as to take full advantage of any moonlight or starlight that would be available. When there was neither, a guy was just plain out of luck.

On the Ed Cotter farm south of Marshall in Lyon County, they had painted the lid that fitted down over the hole on the seat white. That way, if there was any light at all, a person could tell, at a glance, if the lid was up or down. If that familiar square of white was visible, the occupant would have to lift it up. If, however, he saw the blackness of the round hole, he knew the lid was already up.

That all worked real well until one night when Ed walked out to the outhouse. It was a pretty dark night, just a few stars were out but enough to see by.

Ed glanced down and saw the round black hole so didn't bother lifting the lid.

Within a couple of seconds there was all sorts of

racket and commotion coming from that outhouse. The whole thing was a painful and nasty situation, no doublt about it.

I suppose that just about everybody had seen the various ways that a dog will lie and sleep. Like people, they have a variety of positions they will take. A common once, however, is that they will curl around with their tails tucked under their noses and form an almost perfect circle.

Well, that's the way Ruffles, the Cotters' dog, was sleeping that evening, and unfortunately, doing so right on the lid of the outhouse seat. He was snoozing away, just as innocently as could be.

In that dim starlight, Ed didn't see that the black circle that he thought was the hole in the seat was actually his faithful dog, Ruffles. To make a long story, short, Ed Cotter sat right on his dog.

Now Ed Cotter was a pretty fair-sized man, and when he sat down on poor Ruffles, it woke that mutt up pretty fast. And nobody likes to get sat on, dogs included.

Apparently that dog overreacted to the situation. He responded in the only really effective way he knew to the pain of getting sat on. He bit, and he bit hard.

Ruffles was, as I say, just a mutt. Apparently, though, he had enough bulldog in him that he choose to chomp down and stay chomped.

It didn't take Ed Cotter long to sit on a biting dog before he had had enough of that. He came out of that building like he'd been shot, with his theretofore faithful dog still clinging to his backside.

No amount of slapping at that dog was going to convince him to let go. Ruffles had been asleep, not hurting anyone, and got sat on hard. He wasn't about to let the guilty party go with just a little nip.

Ed didn't know it at the time, but that very moment was laying the groundwork for him to learn how to sit on just one edge of a chair for the next couple of weeks.

Ed got almost all the way to the house before his dog figured he'd had enough and dropped off. Within seconds he was headed for under the porch.

They had to call a doctor to tend to Ed's wounds. It took twenty-two stitches to patch him up again.

CHAPTER XIX

JUST TOO DANGEROUS

A four hundred and six foot long outhouse?

Well, no. The outhouse wasn't actually four hundred and six feet long, but it was part of a structure of that dimension.

The whole thing started when Emil and Ola Frinte came to Minnesota from Pennsylvania in the late 1890s to farm.

Emil and Ola had been raised in the "Dutch culture of Pennsylvania.

When this couple came to settle

near Wilmar in Kandiyohi County, they brought, their old German ideas with them. One of these was the way to design farm buildings all in a long row, all under the same roof. This scheme had several advantages. Chief among them was the conservation of materials. Each building tacked on needed only a front and a back, plus an extension of the roof. Both ends would be unnecessary since the "building" was simply an extension of an existing one.

Another important advantage was that a farmer could "walk out" to the barn without even going outside. This was particularly nice in the winter when snow drifts to wade through awaited the farmer without such a building design.

Another plus that this offered was the conversation of heat. Each part tended to warm the others.

There was, however, one major disadvantage to stringing all those buildings out together that way. If one caught on fire, and the fire got out of control, everything would go. It's tough enough for a farmer to lose a building to fire, especially a major one like the house or barn; but when everything burns at once, it can wipe a fellow out completely.

It was always a judgment call, of course. Were the advantages of this plan worth the risk of losing everything to fire?

Well, Emil and Ola thought they were so up it all went in 1894. The house and adjacent barn were first. Then added onto those, all in a row, were a grain bin and an outhouse, followed by a machine shed and a calf shed.

On the other side of the house was a summer kitchen, and finally a screened-in porch. That building, whatever you'd call it, stretched from a couple of pine trees shading the porch, all along the crest of a knoll, across a little depression, and over to another knoll by the pasture.

Apparently Emil and Ola had brought along enough capital with them to purchase the farm and erect that structure all at once.

The building there along that hillside looked all in

the world like a little piece of Pennsylvania transplanted to Minnesota. It suited the Frinte family just fine.

The incident with the outhouse took place quite a few years later. The Frinte farm didn't stay in the family long. The death of Mrs. Frinte in 1901 led Emil to return to Pennsylvania, selling out to Luther Holvey.

Luther was what we'd call a character or an eccentric today. He was a bachelor farmer who lived on the Frinte place for a little over twenty years.

Sometimes during Luther's tenure he made an interesting modification to the building. He widened the doorways connecting all the parts of the structure and replaced the doors with strips of burlap hanging down, much like those modern arrangements wherein strips of clear plastic are hung over a doorway to allow easy passage, yet hold the heat in.

Luther's plan was then topped off with the laying of a plank floor three feet wide for the entire length of the building.

With all the doors gone and that nice plank base, Luther could bicycle from any one portion of that four hundred and six foot structure to another in a matter of seconds. Luther had a real good thing going and was right proud of it.

It was in 1908 when Hans Jervik came to Wilmar from Norway that the outhouse portion of this tale was dramatically played out. That outhouse, and the incident in it, totally changed the course of the lives of Hans and all his descendents.

For some unknown reason, Hans ended up staying with Luther. Hans got off the boat on Tuesday and was living with Luther within a week. About six weeks later the new immigrant had a job and was well on his way to becoming a full-fledged American. That is, he was until he made a short visit to the outhouse.

Hans was setting there minding his own business when those burlap strips from between the grain bin and the outhouse flew up into the air, and suddenly the room was filled with a throughly frighted and panicked four-hundred-pound calf.

That calf was still in the air from his sudden decision to climb the wall of the outhouse when Luther slammed into it with the bicycle he'd been using to chase the animal.

The images crowded into Hans' eyes. He could see flailing hooves, an awful lot of hide and hair veering down on him, and Luther's arms and legs flopping around like those of a rag doll thrown up in the air. All this, of course, in a tiny room where such goings-on all but guaranteed that somebody was going to get hurt real good.

Right in the center of all this was Hans. He hadn't the foggiest idea that Luther had been chasing a calf, much less that Luther, the calf and the bicycle would all end up crashing down on him.

When the roaring subsided and the dust settled, the calf was finally back in the barn.

Luther and Hans took inventory of the damages. The calf was in fine shape, but there were several spokes broken out of the bicycle. There were also somewhere between two and five ribs broken. Luther had what was promising to be a very painful black eye. Hans had a fat lip, a sprained shoulder, numerous cuts and abrasions, and at least half of the broken ribs.

Of the two men, Hans came out the second best. He was pretty well beat up over the incident. He got so stoved up over it all that he found it necessary to stay home from his job in Wilmer for several days. All he did for that time was to loaf around the farm.

On occasion, during that enforced idleness, Hans would stroll out to see the calf that started the whole mess. Calf seemed to have forgotten the ordeal and busied herself with eating.

After several days of this, Hans made the mistake of writing a letter home to Norway. In his letter he told about the "calf in the outhouse" incident and recited a list of all the injuries he sustained.

Mrs. Jervik's reaction was typically a mother's one. She immediately sent him a steamer ticket and instructions to come right home right away.

Apparently, Hans was not accustomed to going

counter to her wishes but sent a second letter suggesting that he stay here in America. He told her of the many things to do and the endless opportunities in the United States.

All that was to no avail. He got a second letter telling him to get on that steamer and return to Norway without delay.

So, that's what he did. He packed up what he brought to America and returned to his native Norway.

Hans and Luther kept up a corrospondence for several months after Hans left.

In one of those letters, Hans explained that his mother insisted that he return and would hear of no talk about going back to America.

"She told me, Luther, after I got home here and she knew that if I could get in that much trouble just settin' in an outhouse, that I would never survive the even more dangerous things that were sure to befall me.

I tried to tell her that it was a simple matter of being in the wrong place at the wrong time, and such a thing would never happen again.

But it wasn't any use. She reminded me of all the Indians in America. She said that if I could get into that much trouble in an outhouse, I wouldn't have a prayer of living through it if I ever met up with an Indian.

So today, there are probably at least a couple of generations of Jervicks running around Norway eating lutefisk and lefse instead of good old American food like pizza and french fries, all because of that outhouse Near Wilmar.

CHAPTER XX

THE LAST WORD

Bob Bolann was a young farmer north of Rochester. He had, among other relatives in Rochester, his Aunt Pauline. This aunt was to play a pivotal role in the outhouse on Bob's place.

Bob didn't have an outhouse for the first few weeks he lived on that little farm he bought. He was much too busy to bother himself with the need to build one, so he didn't. He just went off into the weeds and that was that.

Well, "that wasn't that" as far as his Aunt Pauline thought. She felt it was just plain outrageous that Bob didn't have a decent outhouse there on the farm, or any at all for that matter.

No amount of hounding the young fellow would do any good. She would suggest one over near the oak tree.

"Well, Aunt Pauline, now, that is just too far from the house."

"Then, how about out near the dinner bell?"

"That'd be too hot in the summer, what with no shade, and all."

"Couldn't you put one over behind the grape arbor?"

"No, Aunt Pauline, that would be too close to the house."

No matter what the suggestion, Bob wouldn't be convinced to build an outhouse anywhere. He just continued to use his weed patch and let other people worry about their own accomodations.

Bob and his aunt would periodically argue about the outhouse situation, or rather the no-outhouse situation.

Aunt Pauline hadn't actually been to Bob's weed patch and had no intention of doing so, but she realized one day that that was the answer to the problem. She recruited one of her sons to spend the day out at Bob's one Saturday. She armed him with some string, a hammer, and four stakes with detailed instructions on what he was to do.

Bob didn't quite know why his cousin suddenly wanted to come out for an all-day visit but figured that was just fine with him. He could use the extra help with some hay he had to get in.

Bob didn't know that his cousin had a box in his saddle bags with string, stakes and a hammer. He found out though, after dinner about that box of stuff. Bob had just gone out to the weed patch for a minute when he saw his cousin following him. Bob was just setting there minding his own business when Cousin Don came up to him, laden with that box of stuff. Without a word, Don drove four stakes in the ground around Bob, connected them all with the string, squared that little rectangle up, took some measurements and walked off.

Now, it isn't every day that a guy is settin' there in his weedpatch, and someone comes up and builds a little string and stake rectangle around him.

Bob had plenty of time to try to figure it out but just plain couldn't. Haying that afternoon consisted mainly of Bob Bolann asking his cousin lots of questions about why he was acting so strange.

Don's only reply was a grin.

It was on the following tuesday evening when Bob got his answer. There came Don with a farm wagon. He had another cousin with him, and a triumphant Aunt Pauline primly sitting in the seat between the two boys. Back in the wagon was a brand new outhouse with a big red ribbon on it with a HAPPY BIRTHDAY written on it.

Don drove right on past a shocked Bob, past the lilac bush, and right on out to Bob's weed patch. By the time Bob got there, Don and the other cousin had the outhouse almost unloaded already, fitting the thing right down on those strings still stretched between the little stakes that Don had pounded into the ground.

Aunt Pauline sat there in the wagon with a "I've got the last word" look on her face.

Bob then realized what the previous Saturday's mystery was all about. His Aunt Pauline had built him an outhouse.

Bob had kind of a sheepish look on his face. He knew he had been bested.

"I suppose, Aunt Pauline, that this means I'm not going to get that graphophone for my birthday that I've been hinting about?"

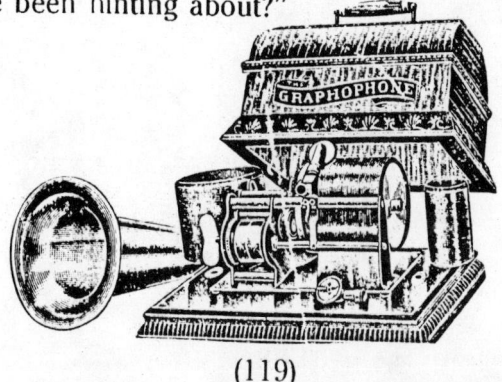

CHAPTER XXI

THE WRONG TARGET

The Ireland boys from north of Jackson were always pulling some kind of trick on each other. One of them would be one up on the other for a few days, then he'd fall victim to a retaliatary trick so they'd trade places. Kirk had pulled one on his brother, Scott, so Scott was layin' for him.

It was on a Saturday while Mr. and Mrs. Ireland were gone for the day when it occurred to Scott how he could fix Kirk real good.

Along about mid-morning Scott sneaked off to the outhouse and poured a little ring of honey around on the seat. He figured Kirk wouldn't see that honey there in the semi-darkness of the outhouse.

It was a good feeling for Scott, knowing that Kirk was eventually going to be going out there. He could just see

Kirk about the time he sat down on that honey. Scott figured that would be a real mess and just about even out the score.

Along about noon Scott went out to check when the boys came in from their woodcutting job their father had left for them to do. Sure enough, that little ring of honey was still in place. There was even an unexpected bonus. Some little red ants had discovered that honey and had a real gold mine there.

All that suited Scott just fine. Those little ants could bite just real good. He knew that when Kirk sat on them he would be in for some real good ant bites. Revenge was really going to be sweet!

Scott half way expected that Kirk might be making a trip to the outhouse during their noon break. No such luck, though. The boys went back to their task without Scott

(122)

knowing the sweet taste of success during that break.

It took longer to saw that pile of wood in the afternoon than the boys expected, and they didn't get back to the house until almost suppertime. Scott had almost forgotten the little welcome-back surprise he had set up for Kirk there in the outhouse.

When the boys got back to the house, their parents had just gotten home. In the flurry of questions Mr. Ireland had about the wood cutting project, the need to carry stuff in from the car and everybody wanting supper, Scott just completely forgot about the honey ring.

Suddenly Scott realized his mother was gone. It was then he also recalled that little trick he had set up for Kirk. With a sinking heart, Scott had visions of those fiery little ants getting sat on by the wrong person. That, of course, could have all sorts of repercussions.

(123)

Scott bolted for the door, just about yanked the knob out of it in haste to be sure his mother wasn't heading for the outhouse.

Just as he got out onto the porch he saw the outhouse door close. The only person it could be was his mother out there.

"Mother! Mother! Wait a minute!"

It was too late, for just then Mrs. Ireland suddenly had an experience she never expected to have that day or any other. A large ring of honey suddenly ended up decorating Mrs. Ireland. Also well glued to her were a couple dozen very, very irritated ants that were more than anxious to wreck havoc on whoever it was that had sat on them.

Mrs. Ireland came out of that outhouse an awful lot faster than she had gone in. Those words: "Mother! Mother!", were still in her ears as she spied her son standing there on the porch looking like he would rather be just about anywhere other than where he was.

Mrs. Ireland was all primed to be real mad at somebody, and she figured she had found just the right person for that.

"Scott, do you know anything about this?" she screamed.

"Yes, Mother. I think I do."

"Well, you had better explain yourself, young man. Somebody is going to be real sorry they messed around with the outhouse."

Scott got a lecture that evening he was to never forget. It dealt heavily with such things as "growing up" "doing your work instead of fooling around," and other such stuff.

When Scott's mother got tired of lecturing him, her husband would take over for awhile.

Mr. and Mrs. Ireland, Kirk Ireland, and all those little red ants are gone now. Scott is an old man who spends a lot of time sitting in the sunroom of a retirement home in St. Paul. He thinks often of the day he unsuccessfully tried to get even with his brother.

CHAPTER XXII

THE TREE-OUTHOUSE

There have been some mighty strange outhouses in Minnesota. One of the oddest stories is that told about in Chapter XXIV made out of blocks of ice.

This story however, is about one I heard about over in Brown County near New Ulm. It took quite a bit of poking around before I found someone who knew something about it. But, I finally found an old duffer who not only knew about the outhouse but had seen it with his own eyes when he was a child.

"It was the only outhouse I'd ever seen that was made out of a hollow tree."

"You sure it was a hollow tree?" I asked.

"Yep, when I was a kid we had a cow get out and my

pop and me had to go hunting it. We ended up on that place with the hollow tree outhouse. I don't know what the name of that family was, but it was those folks that had that strange lookin' outhouse."

With that, the old man proceeded to tell me about the famous tree outhouse of New Ulm.

It seems that a family had moved onto the farm and found they needed to fix up or replace several of the buildings. The outhouse was totally shot, so they had to provide themselves with a new one. It isn't known if this family choose to adapt an old hollowed out tree as a matter of novelty, or if they simply figured it was faster or cheaper than building a new building.

What the fellow had done was to take advantage of a large tree trunk that was mostly dead, and the center had all rotted out. He got in there with a hatchet and hacked away to enlarge the interior, installed a seat, built a partial floor, put in a door and called it a day. Apparently, the biggest job of all was enlarging and squaring off the door way to take a door.

The old fellow didn't know if they had dug a pit under it or not.

When done, the outhouse wasn't a whole lot different than the cartoon type house-in-a-tree that we have all seen in Saturday morning cartoons.

Whatever the reason for such an odd outhouse, the result was lots of talk in the community.

Apparently all the neighbors came over for the sole purpose of seeing the outhouse in a tree. Things must have been a bit slow there around New Ulm for such a thing to stir up so much interest. Several people brought their cameras along to take pictures of it. One fellow even rushed into New Ulm to hire a professional photographer to come out to take a picture of that odd outhouse.

The old duffer who told me about the tree outhouse said that he saw it only the one time when he and his father were there looking for their lost cow.

"I did her a lot of talk about that outhouse in a tree when folks would get together, though. People never seemed to grow weary of talkin' about it."

He went on to tell me that the tree finally blew down, leaving the folks with a perfectly good outhouse, but layin' on its side. Now, of course, there is remarkably little usefulness to an outhouse laying on its side so the owners were obliged to either right it or burn it. They choose to cut the trunk off, push the thing back up, and put a roof on it.

"I head that after they got it fixed up again, they used it 'til they got indoor plumbing. After that, they burnt it down."

I spent quite a bit of time asking around if anyone knew of someone who might have a photograph of the outhouse-in-a-tree, but to no avail. The illustration on page 129 is a representation as best as can be reconstructed from the description by the old fellow who told me about the outhouse.

CHAPTER XXIII

STUFFED SHIRT

Pete Sheldon lived on a farm but never did a lick of farming the entire time he was there. He had fallen heir to a sizable inheritance, so choose to simply quit working. Pete and his family moved to the farm because they liked farm life, he just didn't care for the work involved.

Pete rented his fields and pastures out to his neighbors and busied himself with frittering away his day doing nothing.

This is, he did nothing of much usefulness. He did manage to keep himself busy on one scheme after the other, however. When he wasn't trying to cross a tomato with a squash, he'd be building a dam on the creek, toying with windmills, building a toy for one of the kids, or working on some other one of his "projects."

Some of these projects had a practical goal and some were done just because they were more fun to do than the alternative of not doing anything. It wasn't that Pete had any adversion to doing nothing. He got in his share of that in, too.

A really bad idea Pete came up with one day was to install a little heating stove in the outhouse. A bunch of Mrs. Sheldon's relatives were coming to visit over Christmas, and Pete thought it would be real nice to afford them the luxury of a heated outhouse.

Mrs. Sheldon's reaction to the idea was guarded and tentative appreciation. She had seen enough of Pete's projects go sour that she had certain reservations about any of them. She mentally went through a list of what all could go wrong and decided that, short of Pete burning the building down, there wouldn't be a whole lot that could go awry. She fully expected that when the stove was installed and a supply of wood laid in, Pete would probably lose interest and fail to fire it up. She figured, however, she could take care of that part if necessary. Yes, it just might be a good idea at that.

Mrs. Sheldon was so preoccupied with wondering

how Pete could mess up on that project that she forgot the attraction her two sons had for trouble, or how they could make their own messes.

Since his wife was pretty enthused about the idea, Pete took right off with it. He bought a tiny laundry stove, and set about to install it.

He got the stove set up, ran the chimney out the roof, and even built a small partition so that the heat from the stove wouldn't radiate directly on the outhouse's occupant in that confined space. Pete built a small shelf for the wood, and stacked that shelf with some nice pieces of oak, all in readiness for the week when the company was coming.

The novelty of a heated outhouse got the two boys to thinking about how they could have their own fun with that thing. The older of the two came up with a good idea, so the boys were merrily working out their scheme while Pete was doing his work.

The week of all the company came, and the Sheldons had quite a house full of a variety of different relatives.

The boys soon found one of these relatives to be just the right one to have their fun with. He was a portly old gent who immediately earned himself the nickname "Stuffed Shirt." The boys didn't use that name in front of him or in front of their parents, but did in their conversatons about the fellow and what they were going to do to him.

Contrary to Mrs. Sheldon's expectations, Pete was quite faithful in keeping that little laundry stove there in the outhouse perking along. He got a nice bed of coals going with that oak so the stove would draw well, then he'd pitch in some short sections of old cresote bridge planking. The cresote in that old planking made those pieces burn real hot so that outhouse was just as toasty warm as could be, even in the bitter cold of that December.

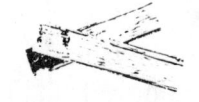

The boys were all ready for Stuffed Shirt and were waiting to catch him in the outhouse. They found their chance one morning along about ten o'clock. Their father had gotten that laundry stove just humming along. He had pitched some of those pieces of bridge planking on the hot coals, and that greasy black smoke was just more than blasting up and out of that chiminy.

As soon as Stuffed Shirt closed the door behind him there in the outhouse, the boys put their scheme into action. They carefully climbed the ladder they had against the back of the outhouse and got up on top of the roof.

That black sooty smoke spewing out of the stovepipe was so thick it looked Like it was liquid coal. Things were working out just right for the boys.

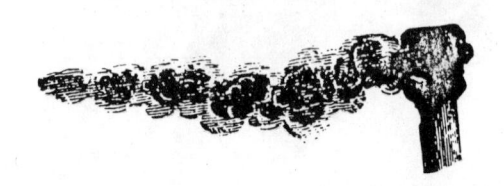

Quickly, the two stuffed a couple of burlap grain sacks down into the stovepipe and then scurried down the ladder.

Those boys had hardly hit the ground when their labors bore fruit. The inside of the outhouse was instantly filled with the smoke that billowed out from under the stove lids for lack of anywhere else to escape. Within seconds, a coughing and gasping Mr. Stuffed Shirt came stumbling out of the door entirely covered with the soot and ashes the smoke had carried on up out of the firepot.

Stuffed Shirt looked like a black man except his teeth

were just as black as his skin. His normally glistening bald head was just as black as the rest of him.

While Stuffed Shirt groped his way toward the house, half blinded, and coughing and wheezing like a freight train, the boys quickly retreived their burlap sacks and their ladder. They scurried off to the barn to put the ladder back and to bury the sacks.

Within a few minutes, the boys came up to the house "to see what all the excitement was about." They joined in with everyone else is feeling sorry for their victim and wondering what could have happened to the stove in the outhouse to cause such a thing.

Pete got a lot of sour looks from Mrs. Stuffed Shirt, along with some pointed remarks over the next few days.

"You'd think," Mrs. Stuffed Shirt would say on occasion, "that a person could have an outhouse that was fit to use. It's a lot more important to have a nice clean one than to have it heated."

For, after the incident with the smoke, the outhouse was all but unusable. Everything in it got covered with a thick layer of greasy black soot. Pete managed to clean it up enough to use, but it sure wasn't as nice as it had been, heated or not.

In spite of all the static that Pete got from the relatives, he was, of course, as innocent as freshly driven snow. He spent a lot of time out there examining the stove and the pipe in an effort to determine what went wrong.

The boys, of course, were very helpful in looking the place over with their father in getting to the answer as to what had happened. One of the pair came up with the idea that maybe there had been a sudden downdraft, what with it snowing later that day, and all.

Pete accepted that as a logical explanation since he couldn't come up with a better theory.

Many years later, when the boys were in their late thirties and figured it was safe to make a full confession, they reminded their father of the "Great Outhouse Smokeout" and 'fessed up to what they had done.

They should have waited another ten or fifteen years to come clean with it all, because the father still got good and mad at them for it.

CHAPTER XXIV

THE DEEP CHILL

Rudy Dana always managed to get along well enough with his brother-in-law, Jep Hillman, to keep from coming to blows, but not much better. Rudy and Jep were simply two different personalities, and the pair always seemed to rub each other the wrong way, so they were always arguing about something.

There weren't any major problems between them. It was just a series of minor irritations and raw spots. The only thing they really had in common was Rudy's sister Mildred who was married to Jep. If it weren't for Mildred, those two would have gladly said good-bye to each other forever.

Jep and Mildred lived in Mankato, and were definitely city folk. Rudy was a country boy all the way to the bone. Neither men thought the life of the other was much to brag about. Jep loved to get little digs in about how Rudy was a country bumpkin and really didn't understand the fine points of how people were supposed to live in the city.

Jep never tired of making comments about Rudy's outhouse and how it was so primative and quaint. He'd make tongue-in-cheek observations on how nice it was that Rudy was keeping an old American tradition alive; the outhouse. He'd point out that if it wasn't for rustics like Rudy, everybody would have to live like he and Mildred - with indoor plumbing.

The outhouse was only one bone of contention between the two men, so Rudy didn't recognize its potential as a means of hassling Jep for quite a while. But one day it occurred to him that he had a perfect way to get back at that smark-aleck from Mankato.

Rudy simply got a log chain around the outhouse and drug it around behind the row of evergreens along the edge of the yard where it would be out of sight. His sister and that rummy she was married to were coming for a few days in January and Rudy was going to be ready for 'em.

After getting his outhouse all set up in its secret place, Rudy proceeded to build a new one on the old spot. This was probably the strangest outhouse ever built in Minnesota, or at least in Blue Earth County. He made it out of blocks of ice he cut from the pond. The walls were ice, the roof was ice, and most importantly, the seat was made of a thick slab of ice.

The whole project took almost two days to complete, but Rudy was really proud of what he had when he was done. Let Jep needle him about his primative outhouse. He'd show that mouthy brother-in-law that primative really was.

Rudy found himself actually looking forward to the day the folks were to come for their visit. There he had him a nice comfy outhouse out around behind the row of evergreens, and all Jep would have would be one very frigid outhouse!

Rudy wasn't real keen on having to subject his sister to having to use an ice outhouse but didn't dare tell her about the real one behind the evergreens. She'd tell Jep, for sure, then all his work would be for nothing. Besides that, she kind of deserved it for marrying that bum in the first place.

It was all Rudy could do to contain his anticipation when Jep and Mildred arrived. He just couldn't wait until Jep made a trip out to what he would be thinking would be the regular outhouse.

The beautiful moment arrived about two or three hours after the couple got there. Jep got up from his chair in the living room, and announced he'd "make a little trip" before turning in.

Rudy did a good job of concealing his real emotions when Jep came back with a disbelieving look on his face. Rudy assured him that the outhhouse was the outhouse, alright. He explained that he thought he'd replace the old one with one made of iceblocks "cause that'd do til spring, and it's a lot cheaper than running out and buying some lumber."

Rudy let Jep suffer through the first day before "suddenly" remembering that he had a ring of fur that Jep ought to take with him to the outhouse, since that was a lot warmer than that ice sheet.

"Ya just set this thing there on the seat before you sit down, and you'll keep nice and warm."

As Jep was examining the fur ring with a skeptical eye, Rudy went on to explain to him that he had made that thing out of any old fur coat and it sure worked well.

Jep didn't know that Rudy had actually made two such rings, one for Mildred which was quite ordinary. The other one was for Jep. The thick fur of that seat-warmer effectively hid the fine itching powder that Rudy had sent away for. That bottle of itching powder had cost Rudy a whole dollar, but he figured he's sure get a dollar's worth of fun out of it.

Rudy was kind of worried, as Jep left for the outhouse, if that itching powder was going to work or not. He had about decided it wasn't because Jep didn't act like he had sat on a powder-puff of itching powder at all for a while.

That night though, it took ahold and Jep was up most of the night doing a whole lot of scratching and carrying on.

Come morning, Rudy inquired as to how everybody slept.

"I tell ya," said Jep." I didn't sleep hardly at all. I got to itchin' and scratchin' something awful in the night. It was just like I was allergic to the mattress or something."

Rudy was glad to hear that Jep was blaming the mattress, and apparently didn't think it might be that fur ring. Maybe he would get another shot at it and manage to put in another sleepless night.

He did.

That bottle of itching powder had been money well spent. Rudy had the satisfaction of seeing his smart-aleck brother in-law spend another sleepless night.

Jep was squirming around in the wagon seat real good right up to the very minute he pulled out of the drive, trying to get some relief from his second bout of itching.

Rudy, of course, "just couldn't understand why Jep was so allergic to that mattress." He assured Jep that he had used it lots of years and had never had any problems with it.

The last part of Rudy's grand scheme took place about two weeks later when he wrote to Jep and Mildred and explained the whole thing. He told him about the itching powder in the fur ring and how he wanted Jep to know that his country bumpkin of a brother-in-law had got him good.

CHAPTER XXV

NO MEAT

Surprise! Surprise! This last story in the book isn't about outhouses at all. It has nothing to do with them. I'm including it in this book, though, because it's a good story and I like it. If you don't like it you'll simply have to put up with it. Besides, I've already gotten your money anyway.

This tale was told to me by my friend, John Gorham, who was one of twelve children back on the farm. John has long left the farm, being a photographer and all, now. The scars of being one of a large family back in the thirties and forties remain, however.

It seems that one day when John was a boy, the family was having some company for supper.

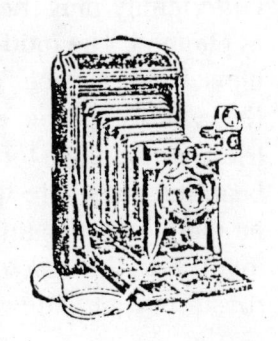

Mrs. Gorham found herself caught a mite shy on groceries, so she took John and his brother, Wilber, aside.

"Now, boys, we don't have enough meat for everybody, so when it comes around you two gotta say you don't want any."

with some grumbling, the pair agreed. It was generally understood that it wasn't in a person's best interest to disagree with Mrs. Gorham.

The hour arrived and everybody sat down; that large family plus the company. Things were just as planned. The food was passed, and each helped himself to a nice generous helping of meat. Everybody, that is, except John and Wilber. He tried not to inhale for fear of getting a whiff of that beautiful roast. He quite casually suggested that he didn't care for any. For one wild moment, he toyed with the idea of spearing a nice hunk of that roast, but he knew better. He could feel his mother's eyes focused right on him. Nonchalantely he passed that plate on to John just as if all it had on it were some carrot sticks.

John glanced idly at the plate and passed it on to yet another brother. Quite coolheaded he was about it all. Not so his stomach. It was frantically yelling to his head to have John drop that nice big piece on the edge off onto his plate. That was to no avail. John had felt the sting of his mother's wrath enough times to know better.

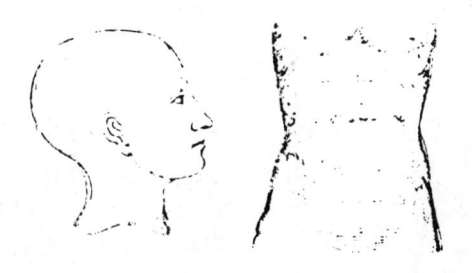

Apparently the boys pulled it off quite well. The meal went without a hitch. Those two boys had some difficulty whipping up a lot of interest in the small talk so typical of mealtime down on the farm. They would have liked to made up for the lack of any meat by wolfing down a mite heavier on the 'taters and gravy, but they didn't. They had been duly warned about that, too.

Soon it was time to clear off the table. Mrs. Gorham quickly did that to make way for the dessert. This hadn't been mentioned, so the boys kind of perked up when they heard their mother getting down those familiar sherbet glasses.

The pair held a whispered conference there at the end of the table, speculating as to what might be forthcoming The duo had spent a long day working on fixin' their father's windmill and they were still hungry.

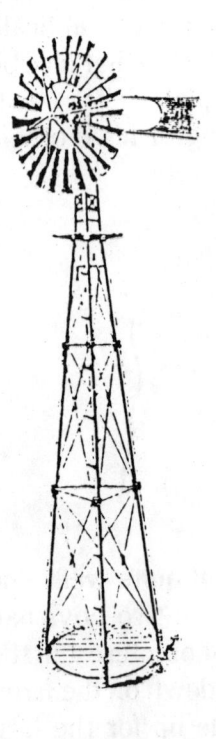

Dessert was always a joyous occasion, but dessert after that meal was nothing less than a Godsend. For what seemed like an eternity, the hungry pair waited for their mother's return.

Sure enough, in a few minutes, Mrs. Gorham came back to the dining room bearing a large tray with a multitude of sherbet glasses, each filled with a strawberry concoction. The boys saw those big beautiful berries flattened against the inside of the glass, all covered with a mound of homemade whipped cream. On top of each scoop of that whipped cream sat another huge berry in solitary splendor. That couldn't have been a more welcome sight to John and Wilber. It was as if everything was all right with the world again.

As Mrs. Gorham returned to the dining room with that treasure, she solved another problem that she hadn't told her sons about. Her problem was that she was a bit shy of dessert, also. Her solution was to enter the room with the following announcement:

"Well, here's some dessert. But anyone who didn't eat their meat doesn't get any."

EPILOGUE

One's heart just has to go out to Cy Cooper when he thought he had lost a new boot down in the outhouse, so he pitched the other one after it. We can really feel for Cy when he found out what had really happened to that first boot.

So it went with life in Minnesota outhouses. Some times it just wasn't fair; like the time when Matt Johnson had to accept the fact that his digging outhouse pits with his fancy machine cost him his grave digging contracts.

Sometimes, though, people just plain would not accept things the way they were and created circumstances more to their liking. One thinks, for example, of Ida from Albert Lea who found it easier to make a new doorway in the outhouse rather than to take the time to find the doorknob. then there was the preacher there at St. Cloud who did the same thing the day he thought the outhouse was going airborne. The poor man didn't know an outhouse from a golden chariot.

Few Minnesota outhouses have been as odd as Rudy Dana's in Blue Earth County or as frustrating as the one at the tavern near Worthington.

If you have enjoyed this book, perhaps you would enjoy others from Quixote Press.

HUMOR:

Iowa's Roadkill Cookbook	B. Carlson	7.95
South Dakota's Roadkill Cookbook	B. Carlson	7.95
Missouri's Roadkill Cookbook	B. Carlson	7.95
Minnesota's Roadkill Cookbook	B. Carlson	7.95
Wisconsin's Roadkill Cookbook	B. Carlson	7.95
Illinois' Roadkill Cookbook	B. Carlson	7.95
How to Talk Midwestern	R. Thomas	7.95
A Field Guide to Missouri's Critters	B. Carlson	7.95
A Field Guide to Iowa's Critters	B. Carlson	7.95
A Field Guide to Illinois' Critters	B. Carlson	7.95

MISCELLANEOUS:

Memoirs of a Dakota Hunter	G. Scholl	9.95
Hitchhiking the Upper Midwest	B. Carlson	7.95
Me 'n Wesley (about homemade toys on the farm)	B. Carlson	9.95
Iowa, The Land Between the Vowels (farmboy tales)	B. Carlson	9.95
Iowa's Early Home Remedies	various	9.95
Illinois' Early Home Remedies	various	9.95
Missouri's Early Home Remedies	various	9.95
Underground Iowa (tales from under Iowa's soil)	B. Carlson	9.95
Underground Illinois	B. Carlson	9.95
Underground Missouri	B. Carlson	9.95
Early Iowa Schools	C. Johnston	9.95

OUTHOUSES:

Iowa's Vanishing Outhouse	B. Carlson	9.95
Missouri's Vanishing Outhouse	B. Carlson	9.95
The Dakota's Vanishing Outhouse	B. Carlson	9.95
Wisconsin's Vanishing Outhouse	B. Carlson	9.95
Minnesota's Vanishing Outhouse	B. Carlson	9.95
Illinois' Vanishing Outhouse	B. Carlson	9.95

ROMANCE:

Old Iowa Houses, Young Loves	B. Carlson	9.95

MIDWEST RIVERBOAT SERIES:

Jack King vs. Detective MacKenzie	N. Bell	9.95
River Sharks & Shenanigans	N. Bell	9.95
Lost & Buried Treasure of the Mississippi	Scholl/Bell	9.95
Romance on Board	H. Colby	9.95

MISSISSIPPI RIVER:

Mississippi River Po' Folk	P. Wallace	9.95
Strange Folks Along the Mississippi	P. Wallace	9.95
Mississippi River Cookin' Book	B. Carlson	11.95

GHOST STORIES:

Ghosts of the Miss. River, from Mpls. to Dub.	B. Carlson	9.95
Ghosts of the Miss. River, from Dub. to Keokuk	B. Carlson	9.95
Ghosts of the Miss. River, from Keokuk to S.L.	B. Carlson	9.95
Ghosts of Johnson County, Iowa	L. Erickson	12.95
Ghosts of Des Moines County, Iowa	B. Carlson	12.00
Ghosts of Scott County, Iowa	B. Carlson	12.95
Ghosts of The Amana Colonies, Iowa	L. Erickson	9.95
Ghosts of Polk County, Iowa	T. Welch	9.95
Ghosts of the Iowa Great Lakes	B. Carlson	9.95
Ghosts of Northeast Iowa	R. Hein et al.	9.95
Ghosts of the Black Hills	T. Welch	9.95
Ghosts of Door County, Wisconsin	G. Rider	9.95
Ghostly Tales of Southwest Minnesota	R. Hein	9.95
Ghosts of Rock Island County, Illinois	B. Carlson	12.95
Ghosts of the Coast of Maine	C. Schulte	9.95

LADIES OF THE EVENING:

Some Awfully Tame, But Kinda Funny Stories About:

—Early Iowa Ladies-of-the-Evening	B. Carlson	9.95
—Early Illinois Ladies-of-the-Evening	B. Carlson	9.95
—Early Wisconsin Ladies-of-the-Evening	B. Carlson	9.95
—Early Minnesota Ladies-of-the-Evening	B. Carlson	9.95
—Early Missouri Ladies-of-the-Evening	B. Carlson	9.95
—Early Dakota Ladies-of-the-Evening	B. Carlson	9.95

INDEX

INDEX

Albert Lea 83,157
Anoka 67
ants 122,123,124,125
Austin 31,95
bees 83,121
Bemidji 77
birds 83,85
Blooming Prairie 95
Blue Earth County 145,157
Bolann 115,118
Brown County 127
camera 130
Canada 48
cantaloupe 32,33
Caseman 73,74
chariot, golden 93,157
chickens 83
Christmas 135
church 41,42,43,45,71,89,93
cistern 95,97
Clante 61,63,64,65,67
claustraphobia 95
Coe 71,73
Cooper 19,20,157
Cotter 100,101,102
cows 26,127
Dana 143,147
DEEP CHILL, THE 143
doctor 73,74,75
DOIN' THINGS BACKWARDS 57
DUAL PURPOSE OUTHOUSE, THE 47
electricity 88
Faribault 35
Fergus Falls 81
fishing 47
flashlight 78
French Fries 113

(163)

Frinte	105,107,108
FROM THE TOP DOWN	25
ghost	35
glue	71,72
Gorham	151,152,153,154,155
graphophone	119
grave	35,41,157
grave digger	41,43,44,157
GREAT OUTHOUSE SMOKEOUT	141
halo	13
Holvey	108
HOMEMADE STORMS	77
honey	121,122,123,124
Hopewell	
Inidans	112,113
Ireland	121,124,125
itching powder	147,148,149
Jackson	63,121
Jenkins	67
Jensen	83,84
Jervik	108,111,113
JOEY'S BAD DAY	13
Johnson	42,44,157
JUST UNFAIR	19
JUST TOO DANGEROUS	105
Kandiyohi County	105
kerosene	51
knife	13,14,15,16,17
LAST WORD, THE	115
lefsa	113
Lyon County	100
lutefisk	113
Mankato	22,144
Marshall	100
Martin	13,15,16,17
MATT'S MISTAKE	41
Metcalf	31
Minneapolis	13,32,41,42
Minnesota	105,107,127,145,157
Mississippi River	48,50
MISTAKIN IDENTITY	99

MIX-UP, THE 31
NEW DOORWAY, THE 83
New Ulm 127,128,129,130
NO MEAT 151
Norway 108,111,112,113
oats 26
Owatanna 53
owl 84,85
Pennsylvania 105,107,108
Penny 95
photographer 151
pig 37
Pizza 113
poison ivy 81
preacher 89,90,91,92,93
Privius Americans 11
rawhide 54
REALLY STUCK 71
Red Wing 48
Rochester 19,115
Romey 77,78
Ruffles 101,102
shaft 87,88,89,90
Sheldon 133,135,136
shingles 26,27,28,29
St. Cloud 71,87,157
St. Paul 57,67,125
steamer 111,112
STUFFED SHIRT 133
tavern 61,62,63,64,65
telephone 37,38
thunder 78
TOO MANY KNOBS 67
TREE OUTHOUSE, THE 127
UNTOLD STORY, THE 81
UPWARD BOUND 87
Vance 53,54
VOICE FROM THE GRAVE, A 35
wallet 58,59
Walpole 25
Washburn 81

Weaver 35,38,39
WHERE'S THE DOOR? 61
Wilmar 105,111,113
windmill 87,88,90,93
WIDE OPEN SPACES 95
Woodward 15
Worthington 61,63,157
WRONG TARGET 121
Year
  1890s 105
  1894 107
  1901 108
  1904 81
  1908 108
  1911 49
  1912 13
  1916 83,84
  1920s 36,77
  1922 19
  1925 17
  1930s 88
  1938 31,32
  1979 71
  1989 11,87

Need A Gift?

For

- Shower • Birthday • Mother's Day •
- Anniversary • Christmas •

Turn Page for Order Form
(Order Now While Supply Lasts!)

To Order Copies Of
Minnesota's Vanishing Outhouse

Please send me _____ copies of **Minnesota's Vanishing Outhouse** at $9.95 each. (Make checks payable to **QUIXOTE PRESS**.)

Name _____

Street _____

City _____ State _____ Zip _____

Send Orders To:
Quixote Press
R.R. #4, Box 33B • Blvd. Station
Sioux City, Iowa 51109

- -

To Order Copies Of
Minnesota's Vanishing Outhouse

Please send me _____ copies of **Minnesota's Vanishing Outhouse** at $9.95 each. (Make checks payable to **QUIXOTE PRESS**.)

Name _____

Street _____

City _____ State _____ Zip _____

Send Orders To:
Quixote Press
R.R. #4, Box 33B • Blvd. Station
Sioux City, Iowa 51109